LOVE
but not lust

By Paul Toyle

9/19/2017

Preface

What is love or what fruits love can bring forth? You may think that's a silly question. Doesn't everyone know what love is? They may think they do but as I'm sure you'll agree, many do not act like they know what love is and the benefits associate with it.

However, I know that love is a huge subject that would take a much larger book to cover everything about it so in order to keep this book short, I elected to cover in the first three chapters definitions and types of love, duties of love, and broken love. For the remainder, I chose some important topics on love that may be on your mind such as:

- Is love important to your health?
- How can you benefit greatly from being a loving person?
- If everyone knows what love is, why then is there so much hatred in the world?
- What's the fruit of love?
- We could conquer the world with love?

I hope you enjoy this book and may you be blessed with love.

Table of Contents

Chapter 1 - What is love?

What is love? You may think that's a silly question. Doesn't everyone know what love is? But do they practice it? Most will say they do but why then is there so much hatred in the world? More on that in Chapter 5. First, let's define love.

Love Defined

Love is one of the most powerful and versatile words in the English language and actually in every other language. The word "love" conjures up many elusive and complex emotions because there are so many meanings for love. Dolly Parton says, "Love is something sent from Heaven to worry the Hell out of you." I think that is very well put but you could also look at love the way Plato did when he said, "Love is a serious mental disease."

If you look up love in the dictionary, you would find several meanings. In the online dictionary of www.dictionary.com, it lists 14 meanings that are a noun, seven meanings that are a verb, and another six idioms. Synonyms listed were affection, devotion, tenderness, fondness, passion, warmth, adoration, and enduring emotional regard.

The number one meaning listed and the most used meaning of love is to have a profound tender and passionate affection for someone. That someone could be a spouse, a girl/boyfriend, a child, a parent, a friend, someone in need, or God.

One of the best definitions of love that I've ever heard comes from an unknown source that reads like this: "Love is like a religion. It's that feeling which can free the birds in a cage, the feeling that can release a man in the asylum, the feeling that outbound all wrongdoings and the feeling that gives wings to your life."

This quote from Dr. Seuss says it all, "We're all a little weird, and life's a little weird. And when we find someone whose weirdness is compatible with ours, we join up with them and fall in mutual weirdness and call it love."

Types of Love

There are several resources that name types of love but to get the names of the basic four types, I'm going to go to the oldest history book there is and that is the Bible. There are four Greek words that describe the types of love — *Eros, Storge, Philia,* and *Agape.* Eros means romantic love. Storge is family love. Philia is neighborly or friendship love. Agape is the Godly kind of love that is shown to someone in need and the type meant in the saying, "Love your enemies."

Romantic love can have several different aspects of love such as infatuation, companionate love, consummate or true love, fatuous or fantasy love, and would include homosexual love. The family type of love refers more to the unconditional love between parent and child and can be one of the deepest loves as anyone who has had a child can testify. The friendship kind of love can be strong especially after knowing someone for a long time. The Godly kind of love would be the kind of love the good Samaritan showed to a stranger who was in need. We see this type of love mostly when a tragedy strikes such as a natural disaster or an act of terrorism. Everyone of the types of love can be strong enough to cause one to be able to die for the other person if necessary.

Is it Love or Lust?

Some people get love and lust mixed up. The best way to tell if it is lust instead of love is to determine if you are fixated on the looks of the other person and that you're more interested in having sex than having a conversation or you consider the two of you to be more lovers than friends. This isn't really love at all and will most likely not turn into love as some may hope. Many people say that when love starts out as a friendship and turns into love, it is the best kind of relationship that would make a good marriage. I tend to agree.

The Need for Love

Humans thrive on love. Our happiness is enhanced by love. Not just being loved but giving love. Needing to give love is just as strong as the need to be loved. Infants only need to be loved and if we don't get loved during the first six months of our lives, we can turn out to be psychologically damaged.

According to Dr. Steinfeld at UC Davis Medical Center, when a new mother responds to her baby's needs, a trust and attachment is started and as it continues, the child learns how to love and will most likely have healthy relationships with others and be able to express their emotions better. You can't spoil a child during the first six months of life. Babies who are held and comforted tend to be more secure and confident as they grow up.

Chapter 2 – Duties of Love

Love is not just an emotion. Most types of love require responsibilities or commitments. I'm sure you've heard of a person with the lack of commitment. Many times this happens due to how the person was raised or they may have been hurt by being in love with someone that left them so it is hard to trust or make a commitment again.

Today's single people seem to be more concerned about finding the right career rather than finding the right partner to love. Unfortunately, they have not learned yet that a career with a corporation does not give you love. They only need you as long as you are productive and will let you go in a second if keeping you is disrupting their bottom dollar somehow.

Loving Yourself

It may sound strange to say that loving yourself is a duty but it really is if you want to have a good love relationship. There are many singles who have not learned to love themselves so loving someone else is difficult. Learning to love yourself usually happens during your childhood and teens but if you have grown up with low self-esteem due to being criticized by family or friends, it will be difficult to love yourself and can actually lead to being abused.

There have been hundreds of thousands of books written on how to build your self-esteem. Most self-help books will tell you that changing the negative voice in your head to a positive one will help build your self-esteem. Many times learning to take care of yourself better, making a list of your positive qualities, and surrounding yourself with positive people will also help. If you feel like you need help or your low self-esteem has led to depression, find a therapist that you are comfortable with for some help.

Love and Dating

The first love is always one to remember. You may have only been in your teens when you felt you had found the one for you but it may not have lasted. It is rare for a high school relationship to last but it does happen and some couples get married staying together for life.

The popular thing today is to meet online and pursue a relationship. There are both advantages and disadvantages to this. Some advantages may be that you can find people who match up with your criteria much faster, you can do long distance dating, and it is a quick way to learn about a person. That is if that person is not trying to deceive you.

Disadvantages are that the Internet is really an illusion or a projection of what type of person you are looking for, rather than what the other person is really like. Not being able to see the body language or expressions on the face makes it possible for someone to totally deceive you with words you want to hear because you anticipate finding the perfect person meant for you when there is no such thing as a perfect person. Video chatting doesn't help that much either since you can still be fooled by lies if that person is a good liar. You may wonder why a person would want to deceive you. They always have a motive that you probably don't want to know about.

Many single people wonder why they can't find a mate. It could be because of several different things but one that is very common is that they are setting their expectations too high so every person that comes along isn't good enough. That doesn't mean that you should set it so low that you attract the low life who will mistreat you. For those of you who make a list of all the things you want in a mate, you may be waiting for a very long time to find them. Having a few things if fine such as similar values, communication ability, respect, trust, humor and a good attitude but having a list that is beyond this is just setting yourself up for failure in finding someone you will give a chance to be the one for you.

Once you start dating a person, beware of anyone who wants to know where you are most of the time or accuses you of seeing someone else as this is a sign of trying to control you. If you are a woman that has been through an abusive relationship, do not tell a person you're dating about it. Some men are looking for someone they think will be a pushover and will put up with an abuser again so until you get to know that a man is not possessive and is trustworthy, keep that part of your past a secret. This advice comes from women who have experienced this type of thing happening.

Another piece of advice is that if you are seriously seeking a mate, tell your date that you are dating just so you can find a suitable mate. This will scare off those who think they can have sex and be on their way but will draw in the ones looking for a mate like you.

Love and Marriage

Most married couples will tell you that the best kind of love is the kind that comes with marriage; however, people are staying single longer today. According to the Pew Research Center in 2012, 78 percent of 25-year-old men had never married and 67 percent of women the same age had not married. By 2016, the median age for first marriage was 29.5 years for men and 27.4 for women, with both saying the primary reason for putting it off was not feeling financially prepared. Economically marriage isn't what it used to be mainly because the single woman makes more money so she stays single longer.

There's a lot of advice on the Internet about how to make a marriage work. Many say that what helps a marriage stay together is having shared interests, having a good sex life, and sharing chores. Those may be true; however, I learned some years ago that the secret to a happy marriage was what is called "The 3 C's." They are communication, consideration, and compromise. Remembering to keep these in mind no matter what the circumstances tend to keep things running smoothly most of the time. This quote from Dave Meurer is so true: "A great marriage is not when the 'perfect couple' comes together. It is when an imperfect couple learns to enjoy their differences."

I do not agree with those who say married couples should fight to have a healthy marriage. Of course, there will be disagreements or even arguments but I don't believe there should ever be raised voices or calling each other nasty names. That stuff is just not necessary and only hurts each partner to the point of losing respect for the other and if you don't have respect, the love will cool off and the marriage may end. Love, respect, and trust are the main components that hold a marriage together. Sex is an important component too but sex without the other three components could become meaningless.

Speaking of sex, it is usually a big part of marriage and keeps it stable and happy, especially in the earlier years together. That doesn't mean a marriage cannot last without sex. If one partner gets sick or when old age sets in, it may not be possible to have sex as usual but if a couple has a lot going for it in other areas, it is possible to stay happy together. Some couples who can't have sex anymore say that cuddling brings on the same type of intimacy and they may even still kid around about sex even though they don't do it.

Extraordinary Couples

Paul Newman and Joanne Woodward had a rare Hollywood marriage that lasted 50 years. They were good friends before marriage and could talk about anything without fear of rejection or ridicule. They had trust and one thing that Joanne truly treasured. She said, "To be married to a man who makes you laugh every day, ah, now that's a real treat." They were well known for always showing affection. A taxi driver said that he had given them a ride once and they were in the back seat making out and giggling. Paul Newman was about 80 years old at the time. Wow, now that's a wonderful marriage!

The most extraordinary couple was a couple that captured our hearts for almost ten years. They were Dana and Christopher Reeve. Superman and Wonder Woman is what some called them since Christopher had acted as Superman and Dana literally saved his life after he fell from a horse in 1995 and became paralyzed from the neck down. He was ready to die but she made a deal with him to try living for two years and so their love was proven over and over while Dana cared for him as he worked to get better for nearly ten years. Their love was very apparent along with the love for their son Will. Dana would always be touching Christopher even though he couldn't feel it.

Dana saw a new purpose in their lives together — to be advocates and humanitarians for the disabled. The Christopher Reeve Paralysis Foundation was born dedicated to finding treatments and cures for spinal cord injuries and improving the lives of people with paralysis. Dana's legacy also includes the creation of the Quality of Life Program to help people living with paralysis and their families. Christopher died in October 2004 and then Dana died of lung cancer in March 2006. The foundation's name was changed to Christopher & Dana Reeve Foundation to reflect the courage and compassion of the Reeves. What a love legacy!

Love and Raising Children

This subject is so huge that it could fill a book so I will just touch on some matters that I feel are important. One of the strongest connections is the love between parent and child. Even though mothers do the majority of nurturing, fathers also have a big impact on a child's upbringing.

One of the biggest things couples with children argue about is how to discipline their children. Some feel it is necessary to be strict and spank or others may be too permissive because they just don't know what to do. Both of those situations may cause the child to have a harder time regulating their emotions and may get into trouble more often. If you can find a happy medium where you guide the child with positive reinforcement, you may be fortunate enough to raise a loveable child but remember that much of how a child turns out is genetics that you have no control over so don't beat yourself up if your child goes astray from how you taught them.

One of the biggest things I wish to stress is how important I feel it is to tell every child how proud you are of them and how much you love her/him individually. And you need to prove it to them by spending time with them doing things together. It doesn't have to be anything that costs a lot of money but it does have to be something that is mentally or physically stimulating and that brings you all a ton of laughter. One last thing, don't keep them away from their grandparents.

If we have children, we can only hope that they will love us as much as we love them. That intense love is hard to describe but I would like to share how the children of a friend of mine were able to convey their love to their mother before she died.

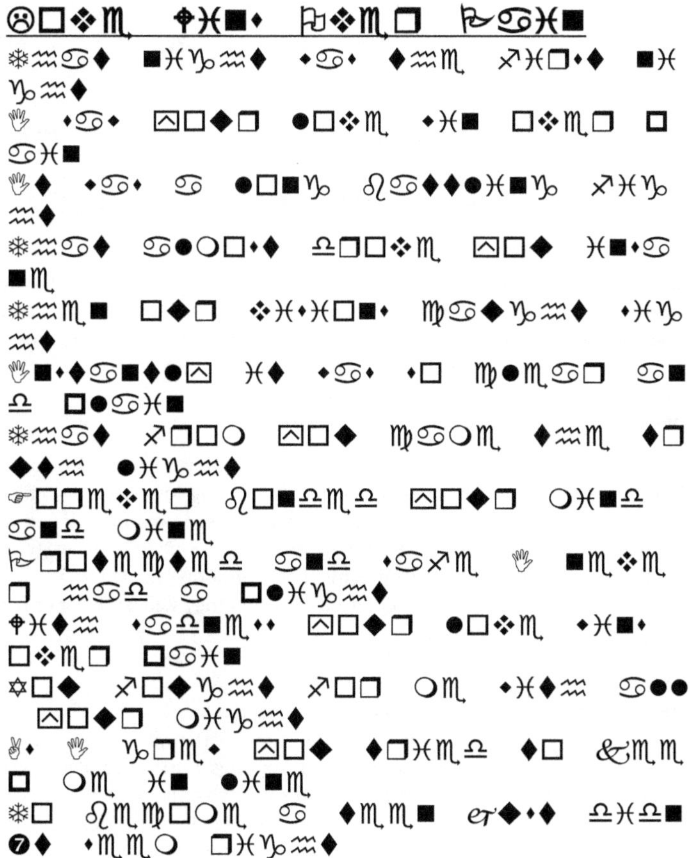

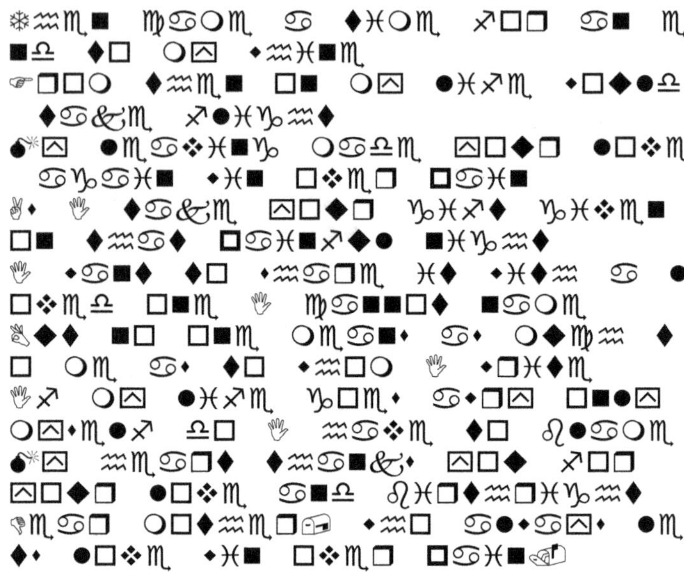

Loving Elderly Parents

Because of our culture and the demands of employment, many elderly parents end up in nursing homes where they are mistreated. If you have elderly parents who need your help, the love you have for them will usually direct you to help them out somehow. When you take care of your parents, you will usually find that it can build up your self-confidence and gives you more strength and courage in dealing with your own problems. However, it doesn't mean you love them any less if you are not able to take care of them.

What I hate to hear about are siblings that cannot come to an agreement to share the load of caring for parents. In fact, I believe that besides saving for your children's education you should also save for the possibility that your parents will need your help. If you do this, then the least you can do is to help them financially or pay for someone to be a caregiver if you're not able to, just to keep them out of a nursing home. This will show them how much you love them and will also be an example to your children for when they will be the ones making those decisions about their parents someday.

Love for Pets

There is a phenomenon known as "cute aggression" that refers to how we love to hug, pinch or express love for others and especially cute babies, kittens, and puppies. Most of us love animals but some have a need to love especially cats or dogs, which usually comes from if we were taught as children to love them. If you had a pet as a child, you will most likely have pets as an adult. If someone hurts pets as a child they will most like hurt people when they grow up, which is usually caused by mental illness or parental abuse/neglect.

Pets have a way of filling a void of love from a human partner. We kid about the cat lady who had ten cats but there is something special that pets give us that humans do not do as much. That is unconditional love. There are various opinions as to whether a pet can actually have love because some believe it isn't love but just being obedient to a master that pets have. It has been proven that the brains of cats are 90 percent similar to ours, which suggests that they could possibly be capable of having romantic love, love for their kittens, and can form a strong attachment to their caregivers. Since an attachment is a form of love, animals such as cats and dogs must be capable of love.

Chapter 3 - When Love is Broken

It is most likely that you will have your heart broken by someone at least once in your life. When it happens, you usually swear you will never love again but eventually most people take the plunge into love again. This is because we realize that we need love and we are willing to take the chance again and again in order to find that special one that will not break your heart.

Love and Abuse

Unfortunately, we may fall for someone who hurts us not only emotionally but physically, verbally, or sexually. It can happen to anyone of any age, gender, race, or economic background. But under no circumstances is it OK to abuse another person. A person who abuses may have been abused as a child, saw others in the family abused, or somehow learned that abuse was OK and eventually will hurt the ones they claim to love.

Abusive relationships are usually based on power and control. The abusive partner usually gets control slowly of everything in the relationship to give them a feeling of power. The victim who is usually the woman tries to understand or change her man but instead becomes in a way brainwashed just as bad as a prisoner of war can be. He may control her by not allowing her to have money or worse, the threat of harm to the children, to her family, or to herself so she does what he says and has a difficult time getting out of the situation.

This type of situation is not love even though they both may claim to love each other. Most victims of spousal abuse can't believe they let someone control them like that once they are free from the situation. However, they need to know that they were not at fault and they should just focus on returning to being themselves and to get professional help if they or any children are suffering from post-traumatic stress.

Love and Divorce

Apparently, the wedding vows do not mean as much to people as they used to since divorce rates are still high and reasons for divorce are numerous. According to DivorceHelp360.com, the top five reasons for divorce are: 1) lack of commitment, 2) too much arguing, 3) lack of communication and selfishness, 4) infidelity, 5) married too young.

Other studies may have found a different list but the main thing is that the love was not strong enough to withstand a few problems and if couples go into marriage without the commitment of it being forever, they can decide that it just isn't working and easily get a divorce.

I found statistics from the Witherspoon Institute to be rather interesting when it came to major factors that determine the risk of divorce for a couple. Some risks are as follows:

- Couples that live together have a 50 to 80 percent higher likelihood of divorce than those who don't
- There is a 14 percent less risk if their parents never divorced
- Having a strong common faith give a lower risk of 7 to 14 percent but if their faith is just nominal there is a higher risk

- The risk is 24 to 66 percent less if the first child is born after marriage
- There is a high risk when marrying a non-virgin
- Believing that marriage is for life protects against divorce.

It may make you wonder if maybe Biblical values are important when it comes to love.

Chapter 4 - Benefits of Being a Loving Person

Love is Good for Your Health

There have been studies done on how good hugs are for your mental and physical health. Hugging can lower your blood pressure, improve your immune system, and release emotionally positive brain chemicals by stimulating dopamine and serotonin. Cuddling and skin-to-skin contact releases oxytocin, which is the love hormone. Hugs and cuddling should not be the only thing that leads a married couple to sex or else if one doesn't want sex then the hugs and cuddling may get put aside as always leading to sex so are avoided and that's not a good thing in a relationship.

Love Standards

Even if not married and you enjoy a single life, there are many benefits of being a loving person. You may have heard this quote, "Love is patient and kind. Love is not jealous. It does not brag, does not get puffed up, does not behave indecently, does not look for its own interest, does not become provoked. It does not keep account of injury. It does not rejoice over unrighteousness, but rejoices with the truth. It bears all things, believes all things, hopes all things, endures all things. Love never fails." (1 Corinthians 13:4-8a *NWT*)

This Biblical quote is how love is supposed to be according to God; however, today most people do not practice love in all of these ways. We can see how love fails all the time by the divorce rate but if more people tried to stick to these standards, perhaps that rate would go down. Some people have some sort of marriage counseling before the wedding day but they don't take it serious enough to make it a subject to talk about at dinner time or any other time for that matter. If couples and families took the time to discuss what helps love not to fail and work at their relationships, I believe that there would be fewer divorces.

Everyone Can Have Love

You may think all the above about love is good but you may be having trouble finding a decent person to love. If you are having problems attracting the wrong kind of person, you should figure out what kind of message you are sending to those you meet or date. There are a few things that will help you do this such as:

- Stick with your values and standards so that others will respect you but you also need to show respect to them
- Show that you have a life with activities and hobbies so you don't come across as needy
- If you complain a lot, act possessive, be moody, or act like a drama queen, you won't attract the right kind of person
- If you are having trust issues, you need to learn how to trust yourself first
- Respect your body and take care of it or else you will attract someone who doesn't respect themselves (both in romantic love and in friendship)

To keep your chances down of attracting a bad choice, pay attention to how they talk about and to their parents. If you're a woman and a man you date does not respect his mother, he may have a rough time respecting you and if you're a man dating a woman who doesn't respect her father, it could mean she will not respect you later in the relationship. Also, if a person does not like pets, they may not be a good choice. Studies have shown that only 15 percent of people do not like cats or dogs. A person who likes pets will be more affectionate.

Love in Comforting Others

Another benefit of showing love to others by comforting them when needed can give you a feeling of joy. Showing love to someone with a broken heart whether it be because they just lost a loved one or they are going through a breakup is a very human thing to do and can have a good effect on both person's mood and well-being. This can be done by just a few kind words, a hug, a gift, or a card or letter. Sometimes it only takes listening to the person's distress or being quietly by their side. This act of empathy helps the person in need feel understood and not so alone and gives us the benefits mentioned above.

Fruits of Love

When you love, the gate of Heaven is ready to open to those who are coming to seek rest after a long journey spent on earth dealing with all kinds of adversity and going through all kinds of experiences that made their faith grow in a way that prepares them for the eternal life. Not only is there a place prepared for them to enjoy life fully with their Creator but their earthly lives would be distinct and wonderfully shaped from all others by the God Almighty.

The things that you can benefit with your own family due to your loving attitude could be enormous. Whether you want to or not, love keeps families together and creates an atmosphere of peace in the house. I know someone who inherited all the inheritance from her grandparent due to simply loving her parent. At the time, her grandparent had a great need of assistance and she was the one who abandoned and sacrificed her own interests and offered assistance. As a result, her grandparent skipped a generation and left tremendous assets for her in a will.

Workplaces do not explicitly advocate love but the kind of teamwork they promote is tantamount to love. Employees who felt they worked in a loving and caring culture reported higher levels of satisfaction. They showed up to work more often. Employees who feel love perform better and stay in the job longer. They commit to the organization, go beyond task of duty, and end up getting raises, promotions and even more.

At school, when the teachers love the students and the student respects and loves the teachers, the learning process goes smoother, faster, and more successful. Students view teaches as secondary parents and the teachers usually go home with the image of the students in their minds on a daily basis. Even slow learner students can feel a great change in their learning process. It was once said by a twelve grade student, "My teacher loves me so much." and she said, "Please always stop by to say hi whenever you get a chance and let me know how you are doing." And she continued to say, "I cannot wait to graduate college and surprise my teacher with a sudden visit. Because she is so proud of me."

We find people who love their church so much, they buy houses close to their church location. They send children to school in reference to their church community. They invest tremendously in the church like their own business. Their primary adviser is their pastor or some member of their church and very often the church becomes their second home. As they are going through life, they are being blessed with all sorts of blessings, not only from God but also from the church members and the church community.

Love is so powerful and immense that a person who never feels love is considered to be dead. The incentives you get for being a loving person is far greater and rewarding than anything that our minds can imagine and someone can explain. Just like plants that need water to grow and flourish, we all need love to survive. It takes courage to love but its fruit is sweet.

Chapter 5 - Conquering the World with Love

What does it mean to conquer the world with love? The word "conquer" makes you think of wartime conquering but the word conquer means overthrow so if the world is overthrown with love, there would be no room for hate.

Why is There So Much Hatred?

The United Nations is supposed to have solutions to the world's problems but unfortunately, too many countries won't put away their weapons as proof they don't want to show love to their neighbor and stop the hatred. On a wall outside the United Nations is a quote from the Bible at Isaiah 2:4 that says, "They will beat their swords into plowshares and their spears into pruning shears. Nation will not lift up sword against nation, nor will they learn war any more." They have had 60 years to make this prophecy come true and conquer the world with love. Do you think they ever will?

We take it for granted that there will always be hate in the world. However, since terrorism came on the scene, we never knew that it could be so bad. The question of why there is so much hatred has been on the minds of many. Most world leaders would blame others by saying it's because of other countries not getting along.

However, the Bible has a prophecy about our time that describes how people would be in the last days. It says, "But know this, that in the last days critical times hard to deal with will be here. For men will be lovers of themselves, lovers of money, boastful, haughty, blasphemers, disobedient to parents, unthankful, disloyal, having no natural affection, not open to any agreement, slanderers, without self-control, fierce, without love of goodness, betrayers, headstrong, puffed up with pride, lovers of pleasures rather than lovers of God, having an appearance of godliness but proving false to its power; and from these turn away." (2 Tim 3:1-5) Many of these qualities could certainly cause the hate we see today. The good news is that it says that we are living in the last days of these types of behaviors. This would mean that God intends on doing something about the hatred and wickedness. If we are open to learning more about it, He will make sure that we will be taught so that we can be saved.

One religious website answered why there is so much hatred by saying that the hatred stems from the Satanic influence that is controlling world leaders, which filters down to their people. Since we know that God is all about love, this could be very possible and if so, it will be up to us to fight that bad influence by doing just the opposite — by loving each other.

Godly and Neighborly Love

"Whoever does not love has not come to know God, because God is love." –1 John 4:8. And if God is love, it stands to reason that we should love God in order to benefit from the love that emanates from him. After all, his son Jesus said the first commandment is to love God and the second commandment is to love our neighbor (Matthew 22:37-40). Bringing this up is not to be preaching at you but just to make you think about it.

If everyone followed those two commandments, there wouldn't need to be any other laws because if we love our neighbor, we are not going to kill him in war or any other time and we are not going to hate anyone. But how do you get the world of millions to do this? The ultimate act of love is to spread the word that the world can only be saved by everyone learning to love God and one another.

A famous man once had some enlightening words that I wish to sum up love with: "Darkness cannot drive out darkness; only light can do that. Hate cannot drive out hate; only love can do that." --Martin Luther King, Jr.

Please check my other books in amazon.com. Simply type Paul J Toyle in the search box.

References:

http://www.dictionary.com/browse/love?s=t

https://www.thoughtco.com/types-of-love-in-the-bible-700177

http://totescute.com/four-types-of-love-greek-style/

https://www.psychologytoday.com/blog/fulfillment-any-age/201308/which-the-7-types-love-relationships-fits-yours

http://www.ucdmc.ucdavis.edu/medicalcenter/healthtips/20100114_infant-bonding.html

https://www.psychologytoday.com/blog/emotional-freedom/201108/lust-vs-love-do-you-know-the-difference

https://www.psychologytoday.com/blog/the-mysteries-love/201402/can-animals-love

http://www.pewresearch.org/fact-tank/2017/02/13/5-facts-about-love-and-marriage/

http://www.alternet.org/sex-amp-relationships/6-extremely-weird-facts-about-marriage

http://divorcehelp360.com/top-five-reasons-couples-divorce/

https://www.psychologytoday.com/blog/myths-desire/201708/the-sexual-science-cuddling?collection=1106047

http://pets.webmd.com/ss/slideshow-truth-about-cat-people-and-dog-people

https://www.jw.org/en/publications/magazines/g200606/peace-on-earth-at-last/

http://www.yourtango.com/2013183005/50-quotes-about-love-authors-artists-musicians-more

Notes

Notes

Notes

Notes

Notes

www.ingramcontent.com/pod-product-compliance
Lightning Source LLC
Chambersburg PA
CBHW061931270726
48660CB00003BA/1134